BLUFF YOUR WAY IN MANAGEMENT

JOHN COURTIS

RAVETTE BOOKS

Published by Ravette Books Limited
3 Glenside Estate, Star Road
Partridge Green, Horsham,
West Sussex RH13 8RA
(0403) 710392

First printed 1985
Reprinted 1987, 1988, 1991
Revised 1992

Series Editor - Anne Tauté

Cover design - Jim Wire
Printing & Binding - Cox & Wyman Ltd.
Production - Oval Projects Ltd.

The Bluffer's Guides are based on
an original idea by Peter Wolfe.

CONTENTS

INTRODUCTION

Management has many facets. It is about style, techniques, theories, functions, tools and leadership. How can you grasp them all? Fortunately you do not have to.

The essence of bluffing is to retain control of a situation, or at least your position in it, without enough data, assets or power to justify that retention. That, as it happens, is also the essence of management.

In some ways management should need no introduction. Most people who delve into this book are exposed to it in one way or another. Even if you are not an employee, every aspect of daily life results from somebody managing something. You may not notice this, because it is only mismanagement which forces itself upon your attention. Late trains? Management failure. Lost post? Ultimately management failure. Industrial action? In the final analysis it usually arises from management failure, now or long past. We are all affected.

It follows that the readership may include hereditary managers, real managers, bluffers, victims and their various spouses. Some are born managers, some achieve management and some have management thrust upon them. You should be profoundly suspicious of those who believe they were born managers, unless their fathers owned the place. Hereditary managers are instantly recognisable by their total ignorance of management, coupled with total confidence. They are only just less dangerous than those who believe their management skills are congenital.

How can a bluffer pass as a real manager? Remarkably easily. Very few managers think enough about their actions, objectives and motives. Anyone devoting even a fragment of the working day to some thought about managing properly can rise above the norm, particularly if he or she displays some evidence of sincerity. On this point we are indebted to Mr George Burns who has been saying longer than any other living Thespian:

'Sincerity is everything. If you can fake that, you're made.'

MANAGEMENT FUNCTIONS

Management teams are split into various functions and the permutations of responsibility are endless. So are the subdivisions in the structure below senior management level. It is important to know what happens in each functional area so you can delegate tasks, objectives and specific responsibilities properly. Bad managers usually need this data so they can allocate blame. Good managers don't blame – they merely find out what went wrong so they can train or plan to avoid recurrence.

The key functions include purchasing, production, sales and finance. In a service or trading company which does not manufacture there will still be an operational core which makes the business proceed and indeed a lot of people call a service 'the product'. People who do this are usually in advertising or marketing. Marketing (*q.v.*) is assumed by sales staff to be part of sales. Marketing people know that sales is part of total marketing.

These and other functions will be explored as follows:

Making Decisions

One of the problems about being a manager is that you feel obliged to take decisions from time to time. This can be very troublesome. However, there are several extremely respectable reasons for avoiding decisions without appearing indecisive.

The first is merely a pair of philosophical quotations: 'If a decision is not necessary, it is very necessary not to take a decision'; and 'If you can keep your head when all about are losing theirs and blaming it on you, you'll be a manager.' They lead naturally to the Kepner-Tregoe theory of problem analysis which suggests that you should not attempt any decisions until you have analysed the problem thoroughly. Most panic decisions address themselves to symptoms and not the underlying problems.

The next line of defence is delegation. Most managerial jobs should involve a high level of delegation to your subordinates. You can buy time and look very professional by delegating large areas of responsibility to subordinates on the basis that they need only consult you about exceptional cases. This is good management practice.

The next problem comes when you are brought the exceptional case. Plan A is to ask "What choices do you feel we have?" and then "Which would you recommend?" because half the time the problem is not insuperable, they just want you to ratify their decision for comfort or security. If they don't have a solution, Plan B is to find out how long you can defer the decision without adverse consequences, in the hope that when the time runs out the situation could have changed.

Meeting

It is said that 'Managers only have meetings when they don't know what to do'. This is not wholly true. Managers also have them when they do know what to do, but don't want to do it; or want someone else to do it, or someone else to suggest it.

Other things being equal, meetings which involve more than two people are inherently inefficient.

8

Bluffers should avoid them. It is easy to disguise your ignorance or explain it casually in a 'one-to-one' situation, but virtually impossible in committee.

Communicating

This all-embracing word appears to cover everything from transport to data transmission. Getting a simple message accurately through a large department is actually very difficult. People read what they want to believe, hear what they wish to hear and generally behave like peasants who have not fully mastered the English tongue and do not plan to.

Good managers have every right to insist that presentations of all kinds, within and without the organisation, be presented in words of few syllables which a child of four could understand.

If you can master the bit about getting information from yourself to other employees successfully, you are ahead of the game.

Instructing

I keep six honest serving men,
They taught me all I knew;
Their names are What and Why and When
And How and Where and Who.'

Kipling wrote it. It's a quotation from *The Elephant's Child* and has considerable relevance in management. It is a handy guide, when you are:

a) preparing a presentation;
b) explaining something in a training or induction session;
c) justifying a major project, or simply,
d) writing a foolproof memo.

Asking yourself the six key words helps you to explain to others, and aids your understanding too.

Managing Time

Bluffers know that management is about managing people and resources. To do this you have to manage yourself. That boils down to managing your use of time. Good managers do this naturally, or by self-discipline. Bad managers never achieve it. Lazy managers may achieve it by omission.

To give a fair imitation of a good manager, try:

• minimising interruptions

• setting aside thinking time

• protecting your diary against inefficient meetings

• constantly checking whether any suggested commitment has relevance to your objectives.

All this helps. The 'my door is always open' management style does not. Balancing the need for a good manager to be accessible, and the need to do some things without distraction, dictates that you be accessible at known times.

Testing for unmanaged time in others is simple – watch for the overtime epidemic. Managers who treat overtime as an extension of the rhythm method are highly suspect. Those who take work home are similarly branded. If you are in a company or department where working overtime is a badge of loyalty or devotion there is no easy countermeasure. You could point out that the Vickers studies in the 1960s demonstrated that output actually falls back to a standard working week after less than four weeks continuous overtime working.

If this does not work, you have two choices. First, to work normal hours, but put in what is demonstrably the best performance; difficult for a bluffer but not impossible. Second, resign.

Accounting

Accounting is a fairly simple process: most of it is arithmetic; not even mathematics. Historic accounts are a statutory requirement and therefore extremely tedious. However, they are susceptible to manipulation. The phrase '**creative accounting**' is a euphemism for tarting up the figures; '**conservative accounting**' is the reverse, still involving manipulation (strictly within the law, of course) to make the figures look less exciting.

Good phrases for a bluffer to use when presented with masses of incomprehensible figures are "Do you really believe the bottom line effect?" and "Is it meaningful to ignore overhead allocation?" This is just credible whether they have done so or not. Their answers will tell you which position they are defending. The real killer is "Can you simplify this so that the board would understand?"

You may also be faced with:

'**management accounts**' – which, because they are generated by accountants, are seldom wholly or even partially intelligible to management;

'**cost accounts**' – which mean roughly what they say; and

'**financial accounts**' which lead up to the 'statutories' in the Annual Report.

Acceptable matters for debate when required to discuss any of these include the extent to which they are integrated one with another. In theory, they ought to be. In practice there are gaps or gulfs of which accountants in particular are well aware. You can usefully ask "How much could this change in the final figures?" The only telling response would be 'These are the final figures' which you may counter with the definitive low blow: "There is never a final figure." This is true, even when the company is insolvent and being wound up.

Analysing Variances

This is what the analysts do with the differences between budget and actual costs, and indeed revenues. The idea is that significant differences (variances) are reviewed, and those which are not the result of incorrect allocation or 'calendarisation' (putting the actual in the wrong period – or guessing the wrong period when the item was budgeted) generate corrective action.

In many companies so much time is spent identifying

the variances that the analysts never get around to telling managers what they mean. You have two choices. Either behave like the tar-baby in Brer Rabbit and maintain a studied silence at some distance from the finance people, or, if you thirst after knowledge and the chance to learn from past errors, go to the analysts and work out together what the variances mean.

Do not accept that analysts know the meaning of every variance. Equally, do not let them infer that management should. This is like either dentist or patient being assumed to have total knowledge of the patient's teeth. The dentist knows what is on the X-rays, and what he or she has observed in the cavities. Only the patient knows what neglect or eating habits contributed to the current state, and which ones hurt like hell. So it is with the monthly accounts. The analysts know what's in there, but you should know the realities of the operation. Between you, you stand a fair chance of identifying problems and the areas where corrective managerial action is needed.

Financing

The corporate finance function varies dramatically from place to place. It is probably at its widest in a merchant bank, where it covers most of the entre-preneurial finance and advisory services provided to corporate clients. It is slightly narrower in the better international banks, loses quite a lot of advisory weight in the clearers, regains a bit of the advisory content but loses some of the funding muscle in the major stock-brokers, and fragments can even be found under this name in major firms of accountants and solicitors, where they are selling advice but no funds.

To confuse matters further, some companies have a Corporate Finance Department which may or may not be the treasury area. Fortunately this makes it legitimate for almost anyone to ask how wide a range of activities any one department of this name provides. Do so and you will look less of a chump than the people who have made assumptions and got it wrong.

Recruiting

Recruiting well is one good way to build a team to whom you can delegate fully and successfully. Most managers recruit so badly that you can be above-average just by avoiding stupid mistakes. The two classic errors are:

a) to assume that a departure automatically leaves a vacancy

b) to assume that you can choose people single-handed.

In practice, a vacancy is a chance to improve the way the job is filled, or to eliminate it. If recruitment is genuinely needed, an extra filter is always helpful, whether it comes from your own team, boss, personnel staff or an outside source. This avoids the problem that personal empathy accidentally becomes the key criterion.

Some very bad managers have become very successful businessmen largely by recruiting with flair.

Delegation

There is a consensus among management gurus that delegation is a key ingredient in good management. Clasp this to your bosom. It enables you avoid many aspects of management.

Once you have a deputy, you can delegate everything from hiring, through induction, training, other aspects of management development and firing, to voluntary liquidation. This last is important. If you cease to be an officer of the company some time before insolvency (or refuse to be a director in the first place) you can avoid assisting the police with their enquiries.

Manufacturing

Sometimes called production, this is a non-essential function, because making things does not automatically sell them. Nearly all companies could subcontract part or all of their production without loss of profit.

Pricing

At some stage in your career, someone in Sales will try to persuade you that the market is price sensitive. True. All markets are to some extent price sensitive, but the basic truth is that all markets are more sensitive to things other than price, unless you are in commodities.

Advertising

Don't fiddle with corporate advertising matters. Instead delegate smartly to professionals. You can then retreat to ignorance as a tactical position which coincides happily with your actual state – but which looks very professional, if not overdone. You can also dispose of the external professionals more easily than internal employees, with less mud shed or indeed bloodshed.

Exporting

'Export or Die' is a much over-rated slogan. Bluffers should regard it as a free choice, with the second option as quite attractive.

Exporting is a pain in the neck. If you are already stuck with it, it may have merits, but plead that you are at the mercy of foreign exchange fluctuations, political uncertainties, legal problems, unwillingness in certain overseas territories to pay for goods and services on time (or at all) and a very high level of overhead which must be reflected in the gross margins.

Even after you have allowed for the cost of distribution, insurance, ECGD cover, warranty, product liability claims, uninsurable losses and selling expenses, there is still the extra burden of the travel bills when sorting out problems or when the relevant director wants to 'show the flag' in the customer territory without any specific sales objective in mind. These trips tend to coincide with major international sporting events.

Procurement

This is a fairly new word for 'purchasing'. Purchasing was a new word for 'buying.'

Buyers are rather important, particularly when they get involved in marketing too, as in some retail operations. This gives them the chance to get it right at both ends. It is not normally noticed until they get it wrong at both ends and the company goes bust.

The textile business is particularly prone to over-stocking problems, as exemplified by the very old joke:

'Would you like a gross of smoke-damaged stock sizes next week?'
'Can I have them tomorrow?'
'No, the fire isn't till the weekend.'

It is not necessary to know anything about buying except that if the staff hold their positions uncomplainingly for too long they are undoubtedly:

a) complacent about new suppliers,
b) under-motivated,
c) on the fiddle,

or all three.

Having to Manage

There will be times when even a bluffer is faced with the need to take a position about something, anything, in management. We have a rule, not a golden one but plated thick enough to pass, which is what bluff is about.

The need to have an opinion will almost invariably involve a flow of data from your inquisitor, who might be subordinate, supplier, boss or customer. The correct posture is the very professional one of wanting to know enough about the circumstances before your volunteer an opinion.

Ask some 'How, What, Why, When Where, Who, Which' questions (*q.v.*), while you are "thinking". Some of these will be answered sloppily. Ask for a more objective input. Even if this is forthcoming, there may be the chance to point out that what you seek are facts rather than opinions. When you get facts, it may be permissible to ask for evidence, just in case the facts are actually opinions.

By this time several things may have happened. Your colleagues may have realised in the process of explaining the situation what the solution is. Or they may have shown that there isn't a problem. Or, by the Grace of God, you may have realised what is wrong, yourself.

Don't think this is just bluff. The process is quite like real management and you will get credit for doing it this way.

PEOPLE IN MANAGEMENT

Accountants

Accountants are often portrayed as dull and boring. This is not fair. In fact, in a survey in 1982, researchers found that a sample of lay (i.e. non-accounting) business people thought that accountants were appreciably less boring and conservative than the accountants themselves assumed. It is useful to be aware of this research material but not wholly safe to quote it to the victims.

As one can deduce from the survey, accountants feel themselves to be unloved. They usually welcome friends in other managerial functions and can prove quite nice to drink with. Do not assume that company secrets will flow after the fifth pint. Most of them did brewery or distillery audits when young and have strong heads. They need strong heads, because they often (not always) know what the company's monthly figures really mean.

Accountants are sensitive creatures who, although they may savage you if their figures are attacked in open meeting, will be pathetically keen to explain them in private beforehand.

Apart from the differences between the major bodies, there are differences in style. Crudely, there are three types. Those who liked doing audits stay on in the profession and you will meet them occasionally in that capacity. Those who did not like auditing spread out through industry and commerce. Many are very entrepreneurial and stop being accountants. Many more wish they could, and join the sort of organisation where they can be called Analysts, Managers, Controllers and Treasurers, indeed almost anything but accountants. If you have this sort, a certain degree of extroversion and indeed management ability can be expected. Companies where they still call all their accountants 'Something Accountant' are probably still rooted in the old bean-counting traditions.

Be nice to the accountants. They wield more power than their image may suggest. Also, they sign the cheques.

Executives

In the USA and now the UK the word 'Executive' indicates a high-ranking employee. In the British Civil Service, which has been around longer and should know about these things, it represents the lower clerical grades. This may tell us something about Business and its knowledge of Government or, more likely, the reverse.

Directors

Directors have statutory responsibilities and power. Alas, they also suffer from a massive burden of legal obligations which can follow them even after they have left the company, or the company has left the lists.

In a fair world, movement from management to directorship should attract a very substantial increase in rewards, as danger money. In most companies, the status is often felt to be more important than the rewards. Even a bluffer should know better.

Marketing People

The marketing staff always know that marketing is the total area concerned with products, services, customers, PR, sales, distribution, advertising and the creation of an external climate in which selling becomes easier or unnecessary.

It is not necessary to understand marketing until it is absent. At that point you may discover that the organisation's marketing was being done other than by the marketing staff. Alternatively, they were doing it, but they didn't know which bits were effective and which bits were not.

If you want to be quotable in this sort of crisis you might point out that Sir Thomas Lipton's comment about advertising 'Half the money we spend on advertising is wasted, but we don't know which half' actually applies to marketing but the word hadn't been invented then. On the other hand, it may be best not to make smart remarks. There are several companies known to us where the marketing staff are merely technicians applying narrow techniques and the real marketing is done by engineering, management, or even buying staff. For the bluffer, it is enough to notice this to be ahead of the game in the next crisis.

Analysts

A job title that is very confusing. To neurotic New Yorkers (finest kind) it must mean psychiatrist. To a few people in real (non-business) life it suggests the Public Analyst, who does clinical things with liquids and indeed solids. In industry today it is likely to mean the sharper end of the accounting organisation, i.e. the accountants who want to be something else and the graduates (MBAs and other) who are passing through finance on their way to somewhere else. In major multi-nationals everyone seems to be an analyst at levels where they are bright but cannot be managers. Do not worry about them but note that they are perceptive and ambitious. It follows that they are likely to be insecure.

Nowhere is this more true than with terribly bright people who have found themselves working for major stockbrokers on the assumption that they must get to the top because they are so much brighter than the partners. There will come a time when they realise that there is only room for one bright partner at a time. Because he drinks less than the rest, it may be some time before anyone can succeed him. Until that time, Analysts will stay analysts, not partners.

You can take advantage of this. Financial analysts in major firms of stockbrokers are incorruptible, cynical, clinical observers of your company. However, if you distract them into a sympathetic discussion of their problems and future, their cold impartial view may be tinged by some element of warmth. Every favourable twinge is a penny on the share price.

Salesmen

The sales function is vital to a profit-oriented organisation. You can exist without most of the other functions, but without sales there is no business. Alas, the sales function is under-recognised. Because it is under-recognised it is difficult to get bright ambitious people to plan a career in sales. Because there are very few bright people in sales the function is under recognised.

This is not your problem. Unless you are in sales, or dependent upon it, this vicious circle does not matter. Stay aloof from the semantic debates about sales being part of marketing and vice-versa. Above all, do not get involved in interviewing sales staff. That way madness lies. They are all above-average, until pressed for factual evidence, when they suddenly become very sub-standard indeed.

If there are no sales staff present you can spend many a happy hour debating whether sales staff sell well because they are thick, or sell well in spite of being thick. The truth is different still. Standards of sales performance previously regarded as the norm can be exceeded by appointing brighter staff unless the product is so pedestrian that the need is really for a charming order-taker and not a true salesman at all.

It also helps to appoint listeners. Selling the customers what they want is a basic principle of marketing. One cannot do this until one has listened to them. Listeners also make good managers. And bluffers.

Finally, no true salesman is going to be insulted by the foregoing, because he knows that he is exceptional, therefore he must be bright, therefore our strictures do not apply to him.

P.A.

These initials can mean 'Public Address System', Personal Assistant, Press Association, Personnel

Administration or Personnel Associates. Guessing which of the last two is the real name of the noted management consultants can occupy many happy hours. All you need to know beyond this is that Personal Assistant comes within the category of non-jobs castigated by Robert Townsend in *Up the Organisation*, although the American term he uses is 'Assistant to'.

All Personal Assistants have jobs without adequate objectives. If they had real objectives someone could devise a real title.

Chairmen

This is one of the few statutory posts enshrined in the Companies Acts over the years, unlike 'Managing Director' which has little recognition in law. He or she is the head of the board of directors, with useful powers and an above-average chance of collecting egg on the face in times of trouble.

The most interesting thing about the Chairman (not Chairwoman or Chairperson) is the Chairman's Report, which forms part of every company's Annual Report to the Shareholders. It is not generally realised that this bit of the Annual Report is not subject to audit and can therefore contain the most utter tosh. Brief review of a random selection will demonstrate that they usually do.

All the bluffer must remember is that the chairman has a casting vote, even if he or she has no shareholding, so time spent briefing or influencing the chairman can be doubly fruitful if you want to further pet projects.

FACETS OF MANAGEMENT

Facets, as distinct from the functions of management, are all the aspects of an organisation which cannot be neatly categorised as the privy concern of one set of specialist managers.

All the things which follow have some impact upon the organisation as a whole, and on the dedicated bluffer in particular. If there is too much emphasis on profits we make no apology. It is not by accident that jargon in the USA now dictates that one asks what the bottom line effect is on matters as far removed as war and sex. The 'bottom line', of course, is the ultimate line on the profit and loss account after all adjustments, good news, bad news and creative accounting. Good management is there as a stepping stone to the favourable bottom line and, apart from one's personal career motivation, profit takes precedence over most other things.

Statistics

All you need to know about statistics is that they are infinitely capable of manipulation and error.

It is no longer funny to quote 'Lies, damn lies and statistics' because everyone has heard it and the impact has gone. Less well known but slightly less powerful is 'He uses statistics as a drunken man uses lamp-posts – for support rather than illumination'.

It is important to remember that all statistics are wrong in some respect. Most samples are biased. Where the samples are not biased, the context in which they are presented probably is. In the rare cases where neither of these is true, the data is likely to be irrelevant to the matter in hand. *How to Lie with Statistics* by Darrell Huff is the definitive work

Profits

These are among the key objectives of most companies.

It is not enough to know this as a broad principle. The way to earn profits and good conduct badges at the same time is to make it clear that you are dedicated to earning today's profit today, this week's this week and so on, because you will not get a second chance.

It is not necessary to live up to this motto, because few management information systems are sophisticated enough to identify daily, or weekly, profits.

Cash Flow

This is important. It is actually more important than profits. Getting money in once you have earned it is vital to survival, unless you have unlimited resources or can use other people's (see Government). Positive cash flow means that the money is coming in faster than it is going out. It does not mean that the outfit is profitable. The money can be coming in because fixed assets are being sold, or because one is reducing stocks to compensate for a declining market. Whatever the case, it is generally a Good Thing.

Insurance

The concept of insurance is fairly well known. If the business is big enough, you may decide not to insure against all or part of a particular risk, rather like the motorist accepting an 'excess' clause in return for a reduced premium.

The process of deciding which risks to accept in-house, and minimising overall exposure to risk, is known as 'risk management'. The process of deliberately not insuring externally is known as self-insurance. The process of accidentally not insuring against a significant risk is known as bad management and can lead to insolvency.

Budgets

These are management tools with which most managers purport to control their areas of responsibility. They specify for a future period the costs, expenses and revenues forecast to arise for a 'profit centre', which may be a complete business or a discrete section of one.

For the new manager the difficulty is that you do not often encounter them first when the relevant period is still in the future. You take over in midstream and then things are even more incomprehensible than they might otherwise be. Acceptable phrases to use while buying time to find out include:

"Did my predecessor actually sign off the final budget?"
"What allocations are in here that we don't control?"
"Are we going to flex the budget for the changes in the market?"
"I'm sure we are not seeing all the costs which are debited against this area. Who is authorising them?"

Even in the best conducted companies most of these will strike home.

Return on Investment (RoI)

A useful yardstick for measuring the performance of a business (or a profit centre) this is an excellent tool to use on things reporting to you, but not so much fun when used against you.

The problem is that all the fixed assets and working capital which look so necessary when considered in isolation suddenly ruin your relative performance, because every excess pound you are using shaves more off your effective return. All those uncollected debts, all the raw materials, work in progress, finished goods, and stock in transit hither or thither, cost money and depress the return. What an incentive to reduce any and all of them.

Tax Mitigation

There are two forms of tax mitigation. One is evasion, which is illegal. The other is tax avoidance, which is legal. In practice, what usually happens is that someone thinks up a scheme and is advised that it is illegal; and then spends large sums of money with expensive lawyers and accountants making it legal.

For the amateur, the best course is to plan to minimise tax liabilities within the law, and also plan to defer the payment of whatever taxes do arise.

It is quite acceptable to ask "What's the true after-tax effect" because far too many corporate presentations make no mention of tax, or treat it as a *fait accompli*. Most corporate decisions have tax implications. Most unplanned tax implications are unfavourable. Being the one who draws attention to the possibility of a pitfall is actually better than being the one who has to describe in detail why the scheme won't work. You get credit for identifying the problem while the poor fish who lists all the Revenue's ways of taking the company's money in such circumstances ends up sounding like someone from the Away team.

Mergers

See Acquisitions. There is no such thing as a merger.

Zero-Based Budgeting

Budgets matter to all managers. Sooner or later you will encounter the zero-based budget development exercise. It is simple and effective. You develop next year's budget without reference to last year's budget or actuals. Human nature being what it is, the exercise can seldom be finished without someone illicitly sneaking a look at the history and screaming about the discrepancies. However, this is inevitable and beneficial. The discrepancies will prove one of three things:

a) last year's expenses or revenues were way adrift of the relevant managers' understanding of them, for reasons which can now be explored, or

b) there are substantial errors of analysis or allocation within the historic figures, or

c) the place could run in line with the new zero-based figures, if management put its mind to the task.

Incidentally, we take it for granted that the new figures are likely to be better than the old. Traditional budget reviews are much too pedestrian to generate positive thought. They are usually concerned with preserving the status quo. Plus or minus 10 per cent.

Loss

The opposite of profit. An unpopular result for your activities. When explaining or planning to avoid a loss, it is politic to remember there are several kinds. A gross loss implies you are selling things for less than they cost, which is fairly stupid. A trading loss implies that necessary overheads have swallowed the gross profit. A fully accounted (bottom line) loss comes after all the fixed overhead and accountants' magic has been thrown in and, although from the shareholders point of view it is still a loss, may not mean trading error.

Value Analysis

Value Analysis means what it says. You analyse the value of component parts of a product, or the whole product. Typically, you will find that the components can perform the same function using less material, cheaper material, less well finished material or less durable material. Components which outlast the rest of the product are inherently suspect.

Sometimes value analysis makes products better than they would otherwise be. The early Ford Cortina is a reasonable example. It was engineered down to a specification in which everything was equally weak, by contrast with earlier Ford volume cars built like tanks. In consequence, it actually proved stronger in use because there were no uniquely vulnerable points where rigid parts of the structure abutted less rigid ones.

We advise using value analysis in other ways. The same technique when applied to services, or your organisation, can work wonders.

Management Succession

This is not a synonym for management development. There are many companies which believe in developing managers but give little or no thought to the question of succession. This is either because they are fairly Victorian in their outlook and assume that you need a few decades before you will have enough experience to be promoted one rung, or because the chief executive is immortal and has no intention of retiring.

Symptoms of the latter include a succession of potential successors who come in as deputy to the patriarch. The former can be tested before you join by asking about prospects and noting whether the interlocutor appears surprised or offended.

Earnings Per Share

To the shareholder, these can be more important than profits or cash flow in that they are the true measure of a company's growth. It is acceptable to be in the 'earnings per share game'. Anyone using this phrase is announcing a worthy objective, while demonstrating that it has not yet been achieved.

Those who have achieved the heights and are up there in the top twenty or so call it the 'earnings per share league' and do so with honour. The rest of us should keep extremely quiet about the whole thing unless and until we are within striking distance of the top. Announcing brightly that you have improved your earnings per share again has the embarrassing side-effect of reminding people (particularly analysts and journalists) to compare your corporate performance with that of others.

Management Buyout

A peculiar deal in which the managers of a business, with or without the help of external financiers, purchase all or part of a business from the proprietors. Usually consummated for the wrong reasons, for if the business is profitable, the managers shouldn't be able to afford it, and if it is loss-making they should have more sense than to buy. It's really like a poker game in that both sides have different views of the business and its future. One or both sides must be bluffing or it would be impossible to agree a price.

Alternatively, perish the thought, the managers are going to work harder, better or smarter for themselves than they were doing as employees. This tells you something about them, or the proprietors, or both.

Acquisitions

Corporate acquisitions are very sexy. They're the ultimate power play.

If you are very secure in your job (Proprietor, offspring of proprietor, major shareholder's boy/girl friend, head of only profitable division) it is possible to be more dispassionate about them. Very few people have the guts to ask, when an acquisition looms up any of the following questions:

- Couldn't we start from scratch cheaper and better?
- Will the customers stay if we buy it?
- Why do they want to sell?
- Why not let them go bust and buy the remains?
- What else could we do with the money?

The last question is best kept in reserve, but any one of these can make you look thoughtful and competent, when all about are falling madly in love with a very suitable partner. Fact: most post-audits of most acquisitions indicate that they failed to generate the profits or other benefits the buyers anticipated. It is therefore good management practice to require to be convinced of the merits of the deal. The correct riposte to anyone whispering 'Dog in the manger' is "Someone has to be Devil's Advocate".

Management Audit

This is a euphemism designed to convince young accountants that they are doing more than traditional internal audit. Ignore it. Most of the time the practitioners are innocuous and won't stray far from the figurework. When they do, their grasp of the business is usually so fragmentary that any findings can be rebutted without reference to the facts and you can then take corrective action quietly after they have left.

Development

As in management development. In its better sense this implies a plan which provides for the progressive movement of promising managers through the company to widen and accelerate their experience. It has also become a euphemism for the 'holding job' so a 'development move' often has nothing to commend it except the move itself. Most major companies even have a special grade for the victims, to permit them to stay on past salary levels while occupying a job graded lower than their previous one. Some development moves are actually constructive dismissal, but there is usually a conspiracy of silence to prevent this being too obvious.

Employees

Employees are very important but they are not the be-all-and-end-all of a business, nor are they assets. Ironically the employment laws seem to recognise this and in their current state actively discourage one from having employees. The legislators have even built in a number of incentives in recent statutes whereby the obligation to comply with legislation reduces as employee strength reduces.

It is useful to point this out to union negotiators when seeking superficial distraction from the main issues, particularly because much of the legislation originated when the Labour Party was in power.

Hobbies

Managers do not have hobbies. They may have extra mural pursuits which help them entertain or interest customers, but never hobbies.

Insolvency

The state of being unable to pay your debts as they fall due. For an individual this usually leads to bankruptcy. For a company the route is via receivership to liquidation. There are however a number of well-known symptoms of impending bankruptcy. Bluffers should keep a wary eye open for:

— Rolls-Royces with personalised number plates
— Fountain in the reception area
— Flagpole
— Chairman honoured for services to industry – every one but his own
— Salesman or engineer as chief executive
— Recent move into modern offices
— Unqualified or elderly accountant
— Products that are market leaders
— Recently changed bankers
— Audit partner who 'grew up with the company'
— Chairman who is known for charitable works
— Satisfied personnel with no strike record
— Recent technological breakthrough
— Whiz-kid as vice chairman

We are indebted to Bill Mackey, ex-senior partner of Ernst & Young, for this list which he claims is a more reliable guide than ratio analysis. We believe it. And would add two more:

— Chairman becomes president of trade association
— Company history published, in hardback.

MANAGEMENT STYLES

Management Styles are generally bunkum. Provided you know the difference between a Theory X and a Theory Y type you know enough. All the theories and other words describe styles. They don't really help you change yours. You can be autocratic, participative, consultative, non-assertive or just plain nasty, but only rôle-playing will change your spots. You can seldom change someone else's.

Fortunately few of your colleagues have been trained to manage. The few who know about it in theory revert to type in a crisis and frequently forget all they have learned, or think it doesn't apply to them. It follows that basic competence as a bluffer will put you ahead of managers trained and untrained. This implies that you may be rôle-playing much of the time. For most imperfect mortals that is the essence of management.

Management By Objectives

A splendid thing when done properly, this consists of identifying objectives in consultation with each job-holder, for each job. You then have a yardstick against which to measure and assist the individual. Even if there is no formal MBO programme, you should be doing this within your own area of responsibility. It will help you to understand your subordinates' work, and help them to understand their responsibilities and the wider goals involved.

If by any chance you are the victim of a bad MBO programme the things which make it bad will also enable you to discredit it. Almost certainly they will include:

a) failure to agree objectives with individuals
b) setting objectives late
c) setting unattainable objectives
d) failure to monitor progress or discuss with staff
e) confusing tasks with objectives.

Genius

This is all right in its place. One can tolerate geniuses at work provided they don't tell you they are members of Mensa. The preferred posture is to have been a member of Mensa but to have resigned when you found the other members were mostly there to bolster insecurities in real life. Being a genius does not make you a good manager.

Innovation

If you are pedalling like mad to stay in the same place, the added strain of innovating products, services or internal systems and practices may not come easily.

We have nothing against innovation. Someone has to do it. From time to time you may wish to do it yourself. However, there is the Better Mousetrap problem. If you have the Better Mousetrap the world will beat a path to your door. Most of us do not at any given time have the formula for a better mousetrap about our persons.

Tactically, it may be better to approve wholeheartedly of the concept of innovation, but shuffle off to someone else the task of implementation. Or else be equipped with reasons for doing it later.

History is well provided with millionaires and innovators. Alas, many of the innovators died penniless. The millionaires tend to be the people who did it second, or eleventh, but properly. An acceptable anecdote in this context is about Andrew Carnegie, the multi-millionaire. His first break came when he had a chance to be a founder proprietor of the outfit which invented the railway sleeping car. Undeniably first, it was not very good so the Woodruff car is not well known whereas Pullman, who did it later and better, is internationally remembered. Carnegie had to make his millions later in steel, doing things better than someone else.

Assertion

Assertion is well worth further study if you want to be professional about your impact on people. Being assertive is described in the book by Ken and Kate Back *Assertiveness at Work* as follows:

- standing up for your own rights in such a way that you do not violate another person's rights

- expressing your needs, wants, opinions, feelings and beliefs in direct, honest and appropriate ways.

It is the counter to aggression and the opposite of non-assertion (being too nice, giving way when in the right, failing to state your case) both of which are out of place in good management and have no place in a good bluffer's armoury.

The best position is to be able to recognise aggression and non-assertion and know they are signs that you can win by being reasonable and firm, against either.

Rôle-Playing

Bluffers pretending to be managers is no news to us. Adults playing at being children are only too familiar. What is less well accepted in business is that there are numerous other subtle gradations of 'act' which people produce consciously or unconsciously during the working day.

Rôle-playing is an essential tool in training activities but the ability to spot it and/or employ it tactically in the work situation, is even more important. Knowing it exists is more than half the battle.

Motivation

Much management theory is about motivation. Relatively little attention is paid to it in practice. It is therefore perfectly safe to know the right names without knowing much about the theories, and then apply common sense in practice. Good practice includes:

a) paying people a fair wage and giving them the chance to earn more, by a known and equitable formula, for above-average performance

b) letting them know the reason their jobs exist and the corporate objective towards which each job is focussed

c) treating them as human beings who want to work and are on the company's side, unless badly programmed or informed

d) promptly praising exceptional effort and achievement, balanced by prompt but tactful guidance when sub-standard work is noted – though not at one and the same time

e) encouraging questions, no matter how basic.

Motivation is like leadership and sex – practise it, but don't talk about it too much.

Management by Exception

A close cousin to delegation, this implies getting involved only with exceptional circumstances. Or things which positively cannot be delegated. Excellent, provided everyone knows it is in use. It goes with clear desks and thinking time.

Appraisal

Staff appraisal is becoming more popular. Avoid it like the plague. The downside risk of introducing such a style, or even operating an existing one, is horrendous, given that it is an open, communicative, democratic one. Good people take their merits for granted and sometimes don't want to know about their demerits. Average people can be demotivated by being reminded how average they are. Below average people can be hopelessly damaged by being told about faults which they do not have the brains or personality to surmount.

MANAGEMENT GOOD AND BAD

The secret of good management is avoiding bad management. Similarly, the test of good managers is that they cannot be observed or remembered for the deviations and idiosyncrasies which make bad managers so memorable. The bluffer, adopting a fairly low profile, is admirably placed to display this symptom of good management.

Good managers don't:

- panic
- abuse staff
- blame people
- get aggressive
- pluck assumptions out of thin air
- fear change
- mistake action for thought
- fall hopelessly in love with the product
- stop learning
- talk more than they listen
- invoke 'necessity' as a reason for anything
- make bald statements*
- worry.

Good management is not necessarily about flair or excellence. It may often be about getting things right more than 90 per cent of the time, by avoiding the crass errors of your contemporaries. This, for the bluffer, must be particularly comforting. Please note that it does not mean avoiding risk. Calculated risk is crucial to business growth. Error is not.

*If they don't know what they're talking about they say the same thing as a question.

Seven Deadly Sins

The fact that we lump the following items under 'deadly' sins does not imply that there are only seven management sins: there are probably about seventy significant ones. But here are a few of the things which managers do, and should not do.

1. Worry

Never worry. If there is something wrong, one of two courses is possible. You can do something to rectify matters, or you cannot. If there is a possible course of action, think about it, explore it, then take it. If not, concentrate on something else you can influence, and the subject of the worries will recede to more manageable proportions. By the time it appears again the problem may have changed, the context may have changed, or your subconscious may have generated a solution. Worry, *per se*, has no place in management.

2. MSU

The Malady of Spurious Urgency afflicts most managers from time to time. In moments of crisis or plain ordinary pressure, there is a great temptation to allocate unreasonably high priorities to matters which in real terms are simply trivial or not really all that urgent. This is a close relation of the urge to be seen doing something in a crisis. The acid test of the true manager under pressure is that he or she is the only one not immediately doing something. The real manager is thinking before acting. Even if it's only a bluff.

3. Weasel Words

In a normal organisation, quite a few people are playing politics. This usually means they are too weak or too devious to get results by normal methods. One interesting symptom is that, although they do not produce outright lies, they generate more than their quota of 'weasel words' in internal documents. The dictionary defines a weasel word as one used to remove any real force from expressions containing it. In practice a weasel word which can imply the opposite of the true meaning is the ideal. A few non-political examples may help. For instance, all qualifying words which prefix titles deserve to be treated with deep suspicion, as in:

Associate Director
Assistant Director
Deputy Director
Divisional Director
Staff Director.

All these carry the message that the title-holder is not a director. Qualifying adverbs are also useful signs of the untruth or half-truth.

4. Spelling

For those who used to worry about 'personal freshness' and what other people think if you order Liebfraumilch, there is something more important: spelling. Those who don't like you will consciously seize upon it as an indication of illiteracy, and those who do like you may subconsciously be irritated that you are letting them down. (It is always assumed that the errors are your

43

own and not those of the secretarial staff.)

There is no excuse, and only one defence – to say brightly when reviewing a suspect text with your colleagues "I think you may have the early uncorrected copy. I don't always spot wrong spelling since I went on that quicker reading course."

5. Thinking the Worst

Relatively few people actively strive to do something damaging or destructive and if they are on your own team, the chances are even slimmer. It follows that when trying to understand the actions of someone else in the organisation, there is usually good reason for them. If the action or the results are actually negative, there are two possibilities. The first is that the corporate context has not been explained to the individual concerned (a classic problem if tasks rather than objectives are delegated). The second is failure in implementing something which started out pointing in the right direction.

The good manager faced with any apparent disaster of this kind assumes the best, but analyses impartially to find what went wrong and prevent recurrence. Bluffers follow suit. Bad managers rush round assuming the worst, allocating blame and generally demonstrating their personality defects to large numbers of colleagues.

6. Being Late

A sin perpetuated by bosses, colleagues and subordinates alike, it is acceptable from none, and undermining in virtually all guises. Worse, it's contagious.

7. Indirect Communications

Mistrust all secondhand communications. Mastery of communications is one of the most useful inter-personal skills in management. If you really want to score maximum points in this area you have to be an aware recipient of communications, not just good at issuing stuff.

Other things being equal, you can guarantee that anyone conveying a message, no matter what their intentions, will in some way distort it.

The classic case is one where all the good intentions run in the same direction. Perhaps you want to order a (perishable) gift to arrive on or just before someone's birthday and you know the someone will return home, at the latest, the day before. If the initiator asks his or her secretary to 'order for arrival on the 30th' knowing that the 31st is the birthday, the secretary with initiative will probably add in a safety margin to allow for the vagaries of the postal system. The suppliers, also used to the faults of the postal system, will therefore receive a request for the goods to arrive on the 29th. Proud of their reputation, they will select a despatch date which makes the 28th the most likely arrival date, with the 27th and 29th as the less likely extremes. This implies despatch by first class post on the 26th. The result is that the goods are going to be unopened and deteriorating from the 26th to the 30th inclusive, whereas without all those good intentions they could have been sent on the 29th to arrive on the 30th or 31st.

Other failures are less simple, but the principle remains – communicate direct or verify direct, depending which end you happen to be.

THE OUTSIDE WORLD

There is a tendency for outfits of all sizes to ignore the things which exist and happen outside the gates. In its extreme form this can lead to terminal megalomania but even mild cases can cause shock and confusion when the peripherals impinge.

An encyclopædic description of all outside forces and bodies is not necessary: most people who are in management can be insulated from them, and those within them (e.g. local government) don't want to read any more cheap cracks than they suffer in the media as a matter of course. Suffice it to say that management in these bits of the outside world includes certain mutations, and one does not mock the afflicted.

Such bodies pay lip service to good management, and genuinely believe they are trying to achieve it, but there is always an archaic rule or practice which prevents them attaining anything but mediocrity in some vital area.

Actuaries

Actuaries are people who would have liked to be accountants but couldn't stand the excitement. They are usually brilliant mathematicians and statisticians, so do not cross them on matters numerical. It is unlikely however that you will meet many of these. Most of them are immured in insurance or pensions outfits.

Fortunately they have little contact with the world of commerce and industry, perhaps even with reality, but if you are involved with the insurance world there is one reassuring fact. Brokers, underwriters and, to a slightly lesser extent, insurance companies, don't know too much about management because they are usually managed by people who know a lot about insurance, and there isn't room for both.

Bankers

Treat with caution. With luck, you needn't have much to do with them. There are only two golden rules.

1. When things are going well and they notice enough to say so, ask them for something. More than you need.

2. When things are going badly, don't ignore them: tell them how things are, and when they might get better. If possible deliver the improvements earlier or better than forecast. This helps them to look good with their area or regional directors.

Bankers are very simple organisms really and quite Pavlovian in their reactions. If you have a choice you should find an optimist. He will eventually get fired or demoted, but in the meantime he provides an easier ride.

Unions

The key point to remember and mention is that an organisation runs on money and people. Managers are there to manage both. Unions only exist because of past management failures and decisions. Making union involvement less necessary is a reasonable target, because its achievement will only flow from good employee relations.

Headhunters

Obviously not small gentlemen with bones through their noses, and acute cannibalistic tendencies. The alternative name is 'search consultants' and as far as we know none of them have bones through their noses. Many are not gentlemen. Some of those who are not gentlemen are ladies. However, they do collect people.

To a headhunter, any manager is a potential candidate, client or source. It is often difficult to tell which way they want to use you because U.K. law makes it actionable to seduce someone away from his or her contracted employment. Headhunters therefore employ a contorted form of approach in which they appear to treat both sources and candidates identically; as sources of advice about a current vacancy. The convention is that if you are interested, you take the initiative and mention yourself. Alas, many people do not understand the convention and mention other people instead.

Some headhunters are suspected of industrial espionage. Others are accused of acting for employers trying to test employee loyalty (or erode it). On balance, even if you were to assume their ethics (*q.v.*) were nil, they couldn't stay in business if they did this often, so it is safe to assume the approaches are real.

The greater deceit is practised by candidates against their bosses. The phrase 'I have been head-hunted' can mean any one of the following:

a) 'I have seen a job advertised, replied to the ad., and not yet been rejected.'

b) 'I have been contacted as a source by someone and am too naïve to know that they want my contacts and not me.'

c) 'I have written to every headhunter in town and one has replied.'

d) 'Nobody has approached me but I am trying to jack up my salary.'

Headhunters are also misrepresented by the press. It makes a better story.

Journalists

Journalists don't have much to contribute to management but you need to watch the press to see what public opinion will do. On business matters the press tends to form, rather than follow, public opinion. The basic rules for dealing with journalists include:

- nominating one person in the organisation to deal with press enquiries; if things are going well perhaps oneself? If not, not.
- presenting the constructive side of things; do not be drawn into discussion on the black side unless you can offer specific and credible contradiction.
- telling the truth
- if you cannot comment, saying why you cannot and when you will be able to; then meet that deadline.
- when there isn't a panic, briefing relevant journalists about the company so that they have accurate background rather than collecting data against time later.

Bear in mind that very few financial journalists have become millionaires.

Business Graduates

Nearly always called MBAs, although the various educational establishments producing them actually issue a variety of degrees, not all of them Master's.

Mature students with an MBA, or equivalent, deserve a little respect. Most have made sacrifices to get them. They are equipped with a wide variety of management techniques and know a lot about the theory of good management. There is a tendency for companies to hire them for their skills and techniques, rather than as potential general managers, and on balance that is probably the right course: they will be better functional managers for their wider knowledge. But entry to and graduation from a business school does not automatically confer the personal qualities and management excellence needed to run a profit centre.

The bluffer needs to pay special attention to MBAs who are the product of part-time evening courses. These devoted creatures spend their nights and weekends studying doggedly and emerge after a few years with dramatically better potential than they had when you first met them.

If you are reasonably successful at work, there is no guarantee that getting an MBA will improve matters further. Some people only go because they are temporarily unemployed or indeed unemployable – a position which may not improve by the time you get out. The solution may be to go on to do a second year, perhaps at Harvard. If you are equally unemployable when that is over, it is helpful to know a few headhunters socially.

MANAGEMENT LITERATURE

Far too much is written far too seriously about management. Even the most arid academic would have trouble ploughing through all the available literature. This glut yields you a bonus in that it is respectable not to have read most of the available rubbish. Being selective in your reading does you credit in this context.

Better still, all management literature is biodegradable. This reassuring and quotable point brings us naturally to other economies of effort. For example, you can be just as sparing in your review of new management theory as you are in other areas of management literature. It is not necessary to be intimate with each new idea. You need only know its name. Then, if the new concept is not just a seven days' wonder, you proceed to phase two, in which you retain an open mind because "it hasn't been validated".

If and when it receives acceptable initial validation, you retreat to requiring large scale practical examples of its worth over a realistic period. 'Realistic periods' when you are on the defensive, are years, not months or weeks.

Phase four is seldom reached, for the delightful and encouraging reason that few new examples of management theory are practical enough for real managers to use them effectively in profit-making organisations. It follows that you can close the book on most of them at phase three, secure in the knowledge that your reputation has been enhanced by considered opposition to the discredited concept. (Phase four, incidentally, consists of finding out more about the theory, once it has demonstrated its durability.)

Names that are always safe to use are Drucker, Parkinson, Townsend and Mead. There is also a superb book written by Kenneth Blanchard and Spencer Johnson called *The One Minute Manager*. It is very short, it uses a large typeface, there is no jargon, and there are very few ideas. But the ideas are repeated several times. Goebbels and Sam Goldwyn had the same philosophy: 'What we say three times is true.'

Peter Drucker is the most likely name one will hear. Fortunately Drucker has written so much over so long a period that it is not obligatory to remember any one chunk of it. The correct posture is to have absorbed it all and forgotten the source. This device is made easier because Drucker lives in the real world and does not need to hang catchy labels on pet theories in order to be remembered.

Blake and Mouton are the correct names to quote in the Managerial Grid context. They are both Doctors. If by chance one gets backed into a corner on the meaning of grid scores, it is enough to know the pejorative ones, i.e:

1.9 = 'Country Club Management' and lacks results orientation
1.1 = 'Impoverished'
9.1 = 'Scientific Management' with human elements obsolete or disregarded.

Professor C. Northcote Parkinson has produced a substantial corpus of light and easily digestible work but is mainly remembered for Parkinson's Law. Bluffers can easily outpace anyone who hasn't read the text recently by asking "Which one?" when the subject comes up, because his first book contains several, and later books add to the score. There is even a Mrs. Parkinson's Law, but unless faced with a rabid feminist it is acceptable, and accurate, to regard this as a pot-boiler.

You will of course know that Parkinson's First Law is *'Work expands so as to fill the time available for its completion'*. But if you are to give the impression of a thorough study of Parkinson, it is important to remember that the Second Law is *'Expenditure rises to meet income'*.

You might also compare and contrast it with Dickens' Mr. Micawber whose views on income and expenditure are well known, but alas most managers are not well-read. Attempts to quote Shakespeare, Wodehouse, Wilde and Waugh can fall on deaf ears. You stand a better chance with Thurber, Dorothy Parker or Shaw.

The Gurus

Management Gurus come and go. Those who stay tend to do so on the strength of their entertainment value, rather than their contribution to management.

There are a few distinguished exceptions, but it will usually be found that their wealth derives from their media exposure and not from their management of successful businesses. They are worthwhile in spite of this because they popularise good practice to an extent that makes overtly bad practice a legitimate target for levity. Many boardroom debates have been disciplined by someone (quoting Parkinson) muttering 'bicycle sheds again', as trivia multiply.

Herzberg and **Maslow** are both in the motivation area. Most people confuse them as they both sound heavy and Middle European. It is enough to recall that Herzberg is about Hygiene Factors, and that Maslow is pronounced 'Maz-love' and is concerned with his Hierarchy of Needs. Other good names include:

Laurence Peter

Peter's mainstream work concerns emotionally disturbed children, so it should come as no surprise that his main claim to fame is in the field of management theory. Bluffers should note that although the theory is Peter's, the man who turned it into a book is Raymond Hull.

The **Peter Principle** is:

'In a hierarchy, every employee tends to rise
to his level of incompetence'.

The corollary is that in time every post tends to be occupied by an employee who is incompetent to carry out its duties.

The Peter Principle, as a book, may be a good example of a parallel principle, i.e. written work tends to be expanded to the point where it loses its impact and thus some, or all, of its merit. For example, a brilliant and pithy concept tends to be expanded into an article or a thesis. A good article too often forms the basis for a book which actually has no extra good ideas in it. This is worst in management literature. Good ideas ought be shortened into slogans.

J. K. Galbraith

Very few economists write well about management. Fewer can write and manage. Indeed there is a respectable body of support for the theory that being an economist actually disqualifies you from managing anything. Galbraith is a respectable exception. He has done much to make economics intelligible to the layman, and even to the businessman.

Perhaps the best reason why he looks more sensible than most economists, apart from the fact that he writes words rather than jargon, is his underlying belief that capitalism (exemplified by American practice) has changed its nature during this century, so that traditional economic theories no longer apply. This of course endears him to all those who hate economists and theories. A useful position.

It is not enough to know that Galbraith exists. You should have read him. The intermediate step is to be able to describe him as the Alistair Cooke of management literature but this is not wholly fair to either although it will do at a party. The book to read, because it is full of cautionary tales about gearing, margins, calls, and corporate collapse, is *The Great Crash*. It is typical of Galbraith that, in the latest edition he reminds prospective readers that book-stalls at airports tend not to stock it.

Shepherd Mead

How to Succeed in Business Without Really Trying produced several worthwhile insights on American management and later was turned into an excellent musical. Mead allows managers to have hobbies, for example, if they coincide with those of the Company President. The hit songs included 'My way is the Company way' and 'I believe in you', a touching love song sung by the hero to himself in the mirror, when he is given the key to the Executive Washroom.

Ivar Kreuger

Kreuger was the man behind the great Swedish conglomerate frauds. He was notable for several reasons. First, virtually until the day he committed suicide he was the darling of the press, public and financial community. Second, he had a useful technique for avoiding issues: he remained silent, playing with his pipe. Few interlocutors could resist the temptation to fill the gap. This is a useful technique, except against Japanese colleagues, who are very patient.

Third, he gained a reputation for being omniscient by mugging up very thoroughly on one subject only before key meetings and then imperceptibly letting the debate slide round to that topic. A bluffer of some stature. We recommend the techniques, not the fraud.

JARGON

Jargon appears to be the major barrier to the understanding of almost any commercial or industrial activity, and most management functions. It would be ungracious to allege that the inmates deliberately seek to obscure their intent by inspired obfuscation, but the effect is as bad as if it were deliberate. The use and growth of jargon was originally intended to achieve precisely the opposite – to clarify and give precision to communication in areas where traditional words and phrases were inadequate. However, the original purpose does not excuse or justify the current results.

When faced with jargon it is not essential to reveal your ignorance, but it is very important to fight back. This may be done, without too much difficulty, by asking that the offending text be simplified to be intelligible to 'lay management', a handy all-purpose phrase, which, according to the circumstances, may include the chairman, new recruits, visiting firemen or the accountant. Here are the key examples.

Behavioural – "Behavioural what?" you might well ask. Behavioural anything is the answer. Whatever is preceded with this word is likely to be a complex phrase for something which seemed quite simple under a much more primitive name, or did not even exist, a decade or so ago.

Bottom Line – The ultimate line on the profit and loss account after all adjustments, good news, bad news and creative accounting. Profit takes precedence over most other things. When in doubt, keep asking "Can we be sure what this is going to do to the bottom line?"

Dedicated – Once upon a time people were dedicated. Nowadays machines are. Anytime you hear that a piece of hardware is dedicated it means the wretched thing is limited in its use. The limitations define the dedication.

Downstream – A word that should have stayed in the oil industry but is being so widely used outside it that you need to know it means the end of a vertically integrated operation nearest to the consumers. Upstream means back at the gusher, or other source.

Ethics – An obsolete term once used in business. You will occasionally encounter it as a warning signal. Anyone professing high or indeed any standards of business ethics should be the subject of profound mistrust. Those who are ethical do not need to say it and, although it may be churlish to remind them, are so only because it is in their long term interests not to be caught sailing close to the wind. Anyone saying 'My word is my bond' falls into this category. Get his word tape-recorded or in writing.

Fiscal – 'Of or pertaining to public revenue', in other words, taxes. Used by people who do not want to mention 'tax'. Find out why they don't.

Gaussian – Nothing to do with the Gauss, which as everyone knows is the electro-magnetic unit of magnetic induction, but another name for a 'normal' distribution of sample data around the average. (Pronounce to rhyme with Strauss.) Also known as a 'bell curve' because it looks like a bell. Tends to be used for effect so treat with contempt.

Headcount – American word for manpower, employee strength, people on the payroll as in 'headcount budget' and 'headcount reduction programme'.

Initials – Management literature and business usage are riddled with initials. They have been since Victorian times. There is no easy way round this. It is not wholly satisfactory to try and memorise all of them, nor is it safe to pretend ignorance. Instead, we suggest cultivating a dislike for initials, because "they can be misunderstood in a crisis". Superficial examination will demonstrate that for every respectable set of initials there is an identical one which means something radically different. For example if you have PC thrown at you it could be Personal Computer, Politically Correct, Post Card, Privy Councillor or indeed Post-Coital. Dr is Doctor to some and Debtor to others; MD is Doctor to some, but Managing Director to us. And so it goes on. A sound excuse for stamping out the jargon of initials and making a name for yourself at the same time. Collect examples relevant to your own environment, or develop some fancy verbal footwork to skate past any queries on this point.

Leader – As in 'market leader'. Market leadership can be good or bad. If it results from innovation, it is conceded to be a good thing, and you should price accordingly while you have the chance. Later, when the bloom has worn off this becomes abuse of monopoly and is a bad thing. Being too big in a market where anyone can copy and undercut is a bad thing unless you are prepared to be ruthless about the competition. (Read *Think*, the unapproved story of IBM.) You can also set up in competition with yourself so you have the two top brands, not just one. Like the cereal and confectionery markets. There are certain markets where it is feasible to be market leader on profit without having to lead in turnover terms. This has very great merits, not least because it is less likely to provoke harsh competitive reaction and price wars.

Logistics – Another of these words where the former definition has not caught up with business usage. The dictionary says 'Art of moving, lodging and supplying troops and equipment' but the drift has been to include all aspects of marketing and distribution including customer awareness. It seems to be applied mainly to 'downstream' operations, not the procurement end.

Management Information – This generic description is applied to any data prepared by non-managers, i.e. accountants, which would not be recognised as being designed or intended for management without such a label. Real managers don't call their information anything in particular.

Mix – We have postulated elsewhere that mix variance is a likely pot for the unexplained variance. Mix itself is a handy excuse for the unexplained profit or loss. It literally means the combination of products you are selling, but usually implies the combination of different gross profit margins represented by those products. Profit that is not as forecast for turnover, even though all other variances are tightly controlled, can always be blamed on changes in mix.

PERT – Another set of initials to mean much the same as **CPA** (Critical Path Analysis) but less well known, if at all.

Proactive – The opposite of reactive. Reactive is what bluffers need to be until they know what on earth is happening, otherwise they become instant members of the zeal-without-knowledge-gang. Proactive is what you should become when you do. You can start testing your proactive responses, and your assertiveness, at the point when you first realise what you are not being told in a report, briefing, or excuse.

Project – Different things to different companies, some of them ominous: a) a capital project, to spend vast sums of money on the development of a new fixed asset; b) a systems project, to spend vast sums of money on a new computer-based system; c) a major revenue expenditure programme. The curse is that each will have contracted the formal description to the single word 'Project', which makes life difficult for newcomers. There are also **Special Projects**, a euphemism for the non job. Any post described as Manager, Special Projects tells you that no conventional job title will fit and that the objective is unclear, except in those cases where it is clearly to find a temporary billet for an unwanted employee. Some of them take the hint, others have to be pushed. A few survive, if their previous merits are not forgotten.

Redundancy – A euphemism for dismissal, these days often genuine. Now respectable, if not endemic, some of the solutions are less well-loved. There are bodies called outplacement counsellors who help victims to present themselves to new employers. There are also those called unplacement counsellors (not to their faces of course) who render their victims unemployable. Their competitors will tell you, at length, who they are.

User-Friendly – A term that has been coined in the computer world to describe any computer/interface which is less complex for the user than it would have been last year.

Vertical Integration – The situation in which you are in control of all, or a large part, of a production process, from the production or extraction of the raw material through to the sale of the finished product.

THE AUTHOR

John Courtis is ideally placed to write about bluffing in management. He has been doing it for years.

He qualified as a Chartered Accountant in 1959 (which conferred absolutely no management competence whatsoever) and was promptly commissioned in the Royal Air Force, spending most of the next three years as accountant officer of a Fighter Command unit on a very remote island. He survived through the good offices of two brilliant sergeants and a devious corporal (see Delegation).

From 1962 until 1967 he was on the finance staff of Ford of Britain, where the foundations of his management skills were laid, mostly by observing others' mistakes. Since then he has been offered (and has accepted) directorships in:

Reed Executive Ltd. (management selection)
Attitude Surveys Ltd. (employee communications)
Executive Appointments Ltd. (headhunting)
Deeko plc (manufacturing).

The common factor in all these was that at the time he joined each board he knew virtually nothing about each business. He assures us that he has learned something since.

He remains Chairman of John Courtis & Partners Ltd., which he does know something about.

THE BLUFFER'S GUIDES

Available at £1.99 and (new titles* £2.50) each:

Accountancy

Advertising

Antiques

Archaeology

Astrology & Fortune Telling

Ballet

Bird Watching

Bluffing

British Class

Champagne*

The Classics

Computers

Consultancy

Cricket

The European Community

Finance

The Flight Deck

Golf

The Green Bluffer's Guide

Japan

Jazz

Journalism

Literature

Management

Marketing

Maths

Modern Art

Motoring

Music

The Occult

Opera

Paris

Philosophy

Photography

Poetry

P.R.

Public Speaking

Publishing

Racing

Rugby

Secretaries

Seduction

Sex

Skiing*

Small Business*

Teaching

Theatre

University

Weather Forecasting

Whisky

Wine

World Affairs

These books are available at your local bookshop or newsagent, or can be ordered direct from the publisher. Prices and availability are subject to change without notice. Just tick the titles you require and send a cheque or postal order (allowing in the UK for postage and packing 28p for one book and 12p for each additional book ordered) to:

Ravette Books Limited, 3 Glenside Estate, Star Road, Partridge Green, Horsham, West Sussex RH13 8RA.